For Leah Damaris,
my daughter

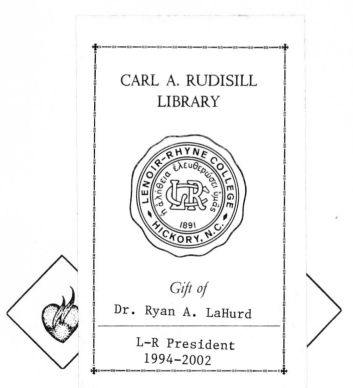

Acknowledgements

25 Minnesota Poets. Nodin Press. 1974. "Sacred Heart, Minnesota" and "Prayer Meeting."
25 Minnesota Poets #2. Nodin Press. 1977. "Policeman."
Milkweed Chronicle. Vol.5, No.1. Fall, 1984. "Curls," "Just Before," "Mother," "Cottonwoods" and "King Tut."
Sing Heavenly Muse! No. 6. 1982.
"Dictionary Drill."

SACRED HEARTS

Poems
by

PHEBE HANSON

1985
MILKWEED EDITIONS
MINNEAPOLIS, MINNESOTA

Library of Congress Catalogue Card Number: 85-61269
ISBN: 0-915943-08-5

Copyright © 1985 by Phebe Hanson

First printing: 1985

Published by **Milkweed Editions**
an imprint of Milkweed Chronicle
P.O. Box 24303
Minneapolis, Minnesota 55424
Books may be ordered from the above address

Manufactured in the United States of America.

Illustrations copyright © 1985 by R.W. Scholes

CONTENTS

FIRST CAR

Here he is in an old photo album,
my Norwegian immigrant father,
newly-ordained graduate of Augsburg Seminary.
My first car—1926,
he has written under the boxy Model T,
familiar car like a child's drawing,
home-made looking,
a car so simple even a child
could drive it,
and I used to pretend,
perched on Daddy's lap,
while we sat in the driveway
waiting for Mother.
Darling and doted-upon first child,
I was stuffed into elaborate costumes,
hair curled and beribboned,
safe in the front seat
between Mother and Daddy,
who drove us to his churches in the country,
Camp Release and Black Oak Lake.
We sang together on the way,
I'll be a sunbeam for Jesus,
I'll shine for Him each day,
In every way try to please Him,
At home and school and play,
that winter night, bitter cold,
snow hissing against our windshield,
the only car out in the midnight storm.
Our dashboard burst into flame;
Daddy disturbed my cozy sleep
against Mother's arm
to rush us out of the car
to stand on the shoulder, hoping
for someone to stop.
That image of the three of us remains,
minister father in long black coat,
mother with fur collar surrounding her face,
child in blue snowsuit and aviator helmet,

as if we were posing for a studio portrait,
as if the swirling snow and relentless wind
were fake backdrops in those old photographs
where the faces radiate a strange silvery light,
and the eyes seem to know that death's ahead
from tuberculosis, pneumonia, diptheria.
We still stand in the bright blizzard light,
frozen images by the side of the road.
I don't remember what happened next.
I don't remember ever being rescued.

TABLEAUX

As that summer when I am three
lingers into heat and boredom,
my mother and her friend decide to have
a little theatrical performance in our backyard
for all the neighborhood children
who want to learn verses and skits.
On the day of the show, my mother
makes divinity and fudge, lays out the pieces
on doily-covered plates in the screenhouse.
All the mothers have been invited,
even Mrs. Blumquist who lies every afternoon,
shades pulled, her migraine throbbing,
thin body flat on her bedspread,
wet washcloth covering her eyes.
I caught a glimpse of her one day
when I was playing with her daughter
and ran in to use her bathroom.
She scared me, lying there like a dead person,
but today she is back on her feet,
come to listen to me recite:
Roses on my shoulders,
Slippers on my feet,
I am Daddy's little darling,
Don't you think I'm sweet?
My mother pulls back the old chenille bedspread
draped over the clothesline to reveal
little girls in tableau, dressed like roses
and hollihocks and pansies in crêpe paper
hats and petalled skirts.

Summers after that,
my mother didn't have time for backyard theatricals;
my baby brother came, then the twins, and finally,
baby from whose birth bed she never got up again,
calling from her room for slivers of ice
to cool her mouth burning with rheumatic fever.
That fall, we all went to Christiansen's Studio
to pose for the family picture we'd never

gotten around to taking before.
There's a place on the bench between my dad
and my brother where the photographer later imposed
an old picture of her,
faint outline of her head and shoulders
glowing above the empty space.

RAPTURE

Bumper sticker on the car ahead of you:
IN THE EVENT OF RAPTURE
        THIS CAR WILL BE UNMANNED.
You hear again your father's sermon
about the Bridegroom
who will come in the clouds
to redeem His Bride, the Church.
You try not to be
like the foolish virgins,
with no oil in their lamps,
try always to be good,
color within the lines
on the blue hectographed sheets
your third grade teacher gives you,
embroider tiny cross stitches
in the dishtowel held firmly taut
by the little wooden hoop.
You even take the pledge
never to let liquor touch your lips,
memorize an oration for the
Loyal Temperance Legion speech contest.

But when He comes,
it is in the middle of the night.
You have slept through
the sound of the rocking chair
where your mother sat
holding your baby brother
when he breathed for the last time
into his new receiving blanket.
*Jesus came and took your brother
away to be with Him in Heaven,*
they told you and they didn't call it
rapture. They called it a name
you couldn't spell when you tried
to write about it in school – pneumonia.
At the funeral, the visiting minister
called it God's will.

SACRED HEART, MINNESOTA

In Sacred Heart, Minnesota,
we Lutherans
barely knew the Catholic kids.
Their mothers smoked Camels,
played bridge in the afternoons
instead of Ladies' Aid.
Their fathers, lying under their Chevvies,
said, *goddamn*, cursing the motors to life.

But we built bird baths of cement,
pressed splinters of broken bottles
into their wet breasts.
Hosiery salesmen driving through
to the Cities marveled.

We gave hoboes
who asked at our backdoors for food
glasses of buttermilk
because it was good for them.

When I was eight, a big Catholic kid asked me
up to his garage loft to see his crucifix.
Even then I knew that Lutherans are justified
by faith alone,
and kept my legs crossed.

11

COTTONWOODS

In the cottonwood grove
behind Dahl's farm
the eyes of rusting cars
stare at me before
I crawl into them,
pretend I am driving;
power flows from the wheels,
I believe I am in control,
forget my mother's heart
lies fading in the little bedroom
beyond the rows of corn.

They have sent me away
from her dying
to play in the grove,
to sit in the old cars,
to whisper into the ears of corn
towering above me
as I sit between the rows
reading her letters
which say she misses me,
even though it is quieter without me
and my brother fighting.
He has brought her a goldfish
from the little pond
beside the pergola house
and laid it on her stomach.

Years later I return to the grove,
where the cottonwood trees
have grown scrawny,
but the old cars are still there,
their eyes stare at me,
unseeing and dead.

CURLS

They told me,
the women who came
bearing macaroni hot dishes:
You must look nice
for the funeral.
They took out the long
curling iron, plugged
its cobra-skinned cord
into our current,
rolled heavy straight strands
around the hot cylinder's mouth
until my long hair
sprang out alive and curly,
frantic corkscrews bobbing
on my puffed sleeves.
But I pulled away
from their soft hands,
ran from them to the sink,
poured palmfuls of cold water
through my curls until they hung
on my neck and I was plain enough
to bend and kiss my mother's hard lips
as she lay in her coffin.

JUST BEFORE SHE DIED

My mother had a vision;
she saw Jesus holding out his arms to her:
Come home, Hildur. Come home.
I know this because my father
wrote it all down
in a spiral-bound memo book
where my mother used to keep
her prayer lists: Ask for another girl,
ask Mrs. Gjerde for forgiveness,
ask for guidance with my sickness,
and her more secular lists:
chipped beef, Karo syrup, vinegar,
long brown stockings for David,
buy Phebe new winter coat.

But I didn't need a winter coat
after all, because the hired girl
who came to live with us
after the funeral
made over my mother's winter coat for me
and said in her no-nonsense voice:
The fur collar's a little big,
but it'll sure keep you
nice and warm.

MOTHER

We listened to strange lullabies
when we were young, sung by our
mother as she lay in her coffin
in our living room. When they
came to move her to the cemetery,
she announced they were not going
to bury her yet, that we must first
learn to honor her dead as we had
learned to honor her alive. Every
morning she sat bolt upright in her
casket by the piano and spoke out
the day's commands. We listened
with respect to her terse words.
It is not easy for the dead to
speak. They are not allowed
to say much, and they must make
every word count. Whatever she
told us we did, because the words
did not come lightly from her tongue.
She had grown less lenient in death,
made only bony demands now, and we
felt the rigor of her presence
until we entered high school and
moved away to the city, leaving her
coffin behind, alone in the empty house.

LONG UNDERWEAR

While my sister is still asleep
next to me in the bed,
I lie awake staring
at the cracks in the rough plaster walls
of our little stucco bungalow.
Outside another blizzard
whips snow against our window,
and no one will go to school today.
But I get up anyway,
the only one awake in the house,
grab long underwear
saved from the day before.
Back then, underwear
was worn for a week,
from one Saturday night bath
to the next.
I race to the hot air register
in the living room,
let my flannel nightgown
drop to the floor,
stand in forbidden nakedness
while the rush of Satanic heat
blasts forth from the coal furnace below.
When I hear the rest of the family stir,
I pull the grey underwear
over my legs,
carefully wrap it
around and around my ankles,
hold it in place with long brown stockings,
stare at the wrinkles,
at the ugliness I won't discard
until spring melts the stubborn snow
of my father's caution,
and lets me wear my legs naked again.

CATHOLICS

I never believed they stored
armaments in their church basements,
or that their nuns weren't allowed
to go anywhere except in twos
for fear they might run away.
I wanted to be Catholic,
like Mary Catherine Murphy,
my best friend all through grade school.
Besides being Catholic,
she had red hair
and was a tomboy, like me.
We both lived on rollerskates
from early spring,
clamped them on as soon
as snow first began to thaw,
leaving little patches of clear sidewalk.
We rollerskated roughly
into all the stores downtown,
even when the storekeepers glared at us.
We were tough, played Kick-the-Can
with the neighborhood boys
far into summer evenings,
even when our mothers called and called
for us to come home.
When Mary Catherine showed me
the picture of Jesus
with the bloody heart luridly extracted
from his body, that heart burning
with an unearthly phosphorescence,
I wasn't afraid at all.

SUNDAY SCHOOL PROGRAM

I drive through the first snowfall,
the flakes a veil across my windshield,
bridal veil my mother kept wrapped away
in crushed tissue in our attic,
soft and gauzy and so fragile
I was always afraid it would melt
when I played with it guiltily
on winter afternoons
while my mother was in the basement
washing clothes
and my father deep in his study
writing sermons.
I would lift out the veil and dress
made of the fabric whose name I found written
in my mother's wedding book:
crêpe de Chine, crêpe of China,
the dress she cut into the winter I was five,
when my father couldn't, wouldn't give her money
to buy me a new dress
for the Sunday School Christmas program;
so she cut up her wedding dress,
made it over for me,
tied around my waist a red grosgrain sash,
topped me off with a bunchy red bow for my hair,
and walked me over to church for the program.
I was so good at memorizing
they gave me the longest recitation of all,
and I had carefully learned it by heart.
By heart . . . .
How many things we learned then *by heart*;
the Sunvold sisters learned all five verses
of "We Three Kings of Orient Are" by heart,
sang them in their deep alto voices,
stood there in choir robes meant to make them
look like Melchior, Casper and Balthazar,
leaned into each other and swayed to the words of the chorus:
Oh, Star of Wonder, Star of Might,
Star with royal beauty bright,

Westward leading, still proceeding,
Guide us to the perfect light, and
their swaying hypnotized me back into summer,
into wondering whether Orient Tar
was anything like the black macadam
that softened in the heat on the road outside our house
until we could dig it out with our fingers
and form it into soft warm balls
that some daring ones were even said to chew as gum.
I was so deep into my tar that I didn't even hear
Mrs. Thorstad, the Sunday School superintendent,
call my name, and my mother had to push me
gently up to stand in front of the altar rail and recite:
If I were just as big as you,
I tell you what I'd like to do,
I'd like to find the girls and boys
Who nothing know of Christmas joys,
And tell them of our Jesus.
As I swung confidently into the second verse,
I'd like to see the manger bed
Where little Jesus laid His head,
And hold His little hand in mine,
And look upon His face so kind,
Delbert Mahle and Leroy Oyum,
who had no desire whatsoever
to hold Jesus's little hand in theirs,
started punching each other and made such a
big commotion I dropped my head
down to look so fast my fat bow almost slipped
off my hair, but I went on reciting
all seven verses, because
I'd gone to a lot of trouble
to learn them by heart and I was afraid
if I didn't finish,
Mrs. Thorstad might not give me
one of the little brown paper sacks
that she handed out to all the children
right before the benediction,
right after all the pieces were said.
Way down in the bottom of that sack was one,

only one, chocolate-covered white cream,
and I always dug down through the bright ribbons
and fat pillows of hard candy
to bring that dark wonder up from the bottom,
to sneak a look at it,
knowing I shouldn't eat it right there in church,
holding it cupped in the palm of my hand,
while I ran the tip of my finger lightly
over the swirl decorating its peak,
then biting into it slowly, slowly,
tiny bites that I allowed to melt on my tongue
and dissolve down my throat,
so by the time my father had stepped up
to the lectern to thank all the children
and Sunday School teachers and superintendent
for the fine program which would certainly
redound to the glory of our Lord Jesus Christ
who came down to this sin-sick earth to be born
in a lowly manger among the humble barnyard animals,
the last of that dark sweet mound had disappeared,
but I still knew it by heart.

BOY FRIENDS

I am in the basement by the old wringer washer
    where my step-mother has taken me
    just before I turn fourteen
    to explain what the blood means.

This is the basement where soon my menstrual cloths
    will lie soaking in the pail of cold water,
    those home-made strips I must wear
    because we are too poor
    to buy the puffy white pads
    I have seen the other girls ask for
    in whispers at Nordstrom's Pharmacy.

Now you must be careful, she tells me,
    when boys try to kiss you.

I remember Darrell's sullen lips,
    Darrell my first Luther League love,
    under the dim light of the church chandeliers,
    sitting together in the back row,
    singing the old choruses:
    Leaning, leaning, safe and secure from all alarms;
    Leaning, leaning, leaning on the everlasting arms.

Later he tries to kiss me under the soft street light
    as we sit in the car before
    he delivers me back to my step-mother.
    Darrell's lips closing in on mine,
    his body pushing hard against my breasts.

If I keep my lips pressed tightly together,
    if I keep his tongue outside of my mouth,
    will I be safe,
    will my blood not dry up?

In the second grade when I was a hall monitor,
    paired with Leroy Oyum, the boy I had a crush on,
    we sat together on the top of the stairs that led
    to the dark basement where the lavatories waited.

We kissed each other's small mouths, unafraid,
    our lips touching with simple pleasure,
    our blood moving fast through our innocent bodies.

INTO MY HEART
for JoAnne Helene (1933 – 1948)

Your fifty-second birthday,
I tell my friends at lunch,
and they smile dutifully,
perhaps embarrassed I would
bring you up, dead these thirty-eight years,
but you are still in my heart,
sister whose picture I took
that afternoon you posed
in halter and shorts
with your friend Suzanne
tanning your skin in our backyard
the last day of summer vacation.
You told me that night as we lay in bed,
you were afraid to go to high school,
that it would be scary in the city
after eight years in your one-room school,
and I fell asleep trying to comfort you.
At midnight you awakened
crying over a headache so bad
you had to throw up again and again.
Next I knew, Daddy was leaning
over the bed to tell me
he was taking you to the hospital.
You had trouble breathing,
and they carried you into our old car
while I watched from the bedroom window.
Your heart gave out because of damage
we hadn't known about
from childhood scarlet fever.
At the funeral we sang
the Bible Camp chorus you'd been singing
with Suzanne just before
I took your picture:
Come into my heart, Lord Jesus,
Come in to stay, come in today,
Come into my heart, Lord Jesus.

23

PRAYER MEETING

There is a fountain filled with blood,
Drawn from Emmanuel's veins,
And sinners plunged beneath that flood,
Lose all their guilty stains.

We sing sitting in a circle on folding chairs
at Wednesday night prayer meeting where fourteen women
have gathered to pray and testify with my minister father.
There is one other man, too old and crazy to be counted,
who jumps up from time to time and shouts:
I'm just an old sinner, saved by grace!
He sneaks me always a hard white peppermint
from a dirty, crushed brown paper bag.
Surely tonight the powerful mint will strengthen
my mouth when it is my turn to speak out for the Lord.
Surely tonight I will not disappoint them.

When the singing is over and it is time to pray,
we drop to our knees in front of our chairs,
folded hands pressed against our bowed heads.
There are prayers as always for me, the little sister
in our midst, a stubborn and difficult child, motherless.
Only the Lord can save her, make her His true child,
if she will repent and forsake her willful ways.

The peppermint grows stronger as it dissolves
like a thick communion wafer on my trembling tongue.
Soon it will be my turn, I who have said nothing
after they have prayed for me week after week.
Some have even cried, remembering the day
my dear mother went home to be with Jesus.

I open my eyes, see through my intertwined fingers
only the eyes of my father, open, looking
at me, waiting for me to speak at last.
I hear my shaky voice rise faint and unfamiliar.
I am saying I hope Jesus will forgive me for
all the bad things I have done and all the times

24

I fought with my brother when my mother was sick
and trying to rest and how instead she got sicker
and then she died even though I prayed and promised
never to be bad again if Jesus wouldn't take her
away to be with Him in heaven.

Now I am sobbing and shaking, and all the women
rush over to touch me and cry: *Praise Jesus!*
He has saved our little sister tonight! Praise Jesus!

The peppermint man reaches into his pocket,
looks away as he hands me the candy.

MODEL A

That was the car we bought
right after World War II,
the old 1931 Model A Ford.
How I hated that car,
embarrassed having to ride
to church in it.
Such a regression it seemed
after the war when everything
was supposed to be better,
everything somehow set right.
Hadn't Mrs. Eddy, our world history teacher,
told us so when we did those projects
called OUR POST-WAR WORLD?
Oh, our brave faith in Dumbarton Oaks,
the United Nations, our revered leaders
of the new one world,
Roosevelt, Churchill, and Stalin!
All the girls I knew then
at Murray High School drove cars –
Maxine, Corrine, Dagny,
and Leslie, so popular she could
get away with a boy's name.
I wasn't in her crowd, but once
she actually spoke to me
in the girls' bathroom,
told me my hair was pretty,
looked like Veronica Lake's,
but I'd look better if I wore
a little lipstick, said as she
smoothed dark red over her own
wide self-assured lips.
Those girls tossed their page-boy hair
against angora-sweatered shoulders,
started up their fathers' cars
and drove off confidently after school
to have cokes at Miller's Drug Store.
My father never let me use his car,
never taught me how to drive,

26

said I could wait until I'd graduated
from Augsburg College and gotten a teaching job:
No point in learning how to drive until
you have your own money to buy yourself a car—
that's the way I did it.
He had my life all planned out to be
very much like his, except I wouldn't go
into the ministry because I was a girl, I'd teach instead,
and then maybe marry a minister who would
drive me from church to church
the way he used to.

PICKUP TRUCK

I'm afraid in the new high school because there are more kids here than in the entire town of Sacred Heart. My clothes aren't right, either. All the others wear penny loafers or saddle shoes, while I must wear the sensible brown oxfords my parents firmly believe are good for my feet. I walk down the endlessly long halls, my body close to the lockers, books and notebooks pressed against my breasts, so no one can see me. Only when I get to Latin class do I feel safe; Mrs. Halvorsen's white wavy hair and warm smile comfort me.

I walk alone to school the two and a half miles down Larpenteur from Snelling to Cleveland, then past the U farm campus and into St. Anthony Park. I always leave while it is still dark, before anyone else gets up, before I have to face the injunctions of my father about coming straight home from school.

I am waiting on Larpenteur and Snelling one morning for the light to change, when a pickup truck stops. A man leans out, asks if I want a ride. I hesitate, but get in. I am used to Sacred Heart where there are no strangers. It doesn't occur to me I can refuse. Besides, the man is old, harmless as a farmer in his visored cap, plaid wool mackinaw, rough and honest. He asks me where I am going, and I tell him Murray High. He says he always drives this way, will give me a ride any day. It's a long way for a young girl to walk so early in the morning. When I tell him my name, he says he knows my father, has even been to his church once.

I ride with him all that fall. He even starts to pick me up in front of my house. My parents approve. They think they remember the time he came to church. I can't remember what we talk about in the truck or even if we talk much. Mostly I stare straight ahead while he drives, but occasionally I glance at his hands on the wheel with their jagged dirty nails. I'd rather ride with him, though, than walk the long cold miles alone.

The day before Christmas vacation, as we near the school, I tell him I won't be riding for two weeks. He pulls the truck to a stop in front of the school. Still dark out with light snow falling across the windshield. He leans toward me slightly, suggests that perhaps since I won't be seeing him for awhile, I might kiss him goodbye. He pulls me against his scratchy jacket. I think I shouldn't resist. He has, after all, been to my father's church, is just a friendly, fatherly man who likes me as a daughter. But my heart roars with fear and my books fall to the floor as he pulls me close to his face. I smell his tobacco when his wet mouth pushes into mine, his tongue insistent against my teeth. How can I stop him, this good, fatherly man?

I struggle to get away from his grasp, and my hair catches on a button of his jacket. I reach down to the floor for my books and papers, open the door and call a weak goodbye, polite even in my fear.

No one has kissed me that way before. I am wild with shame as I race into the school building, push open the door of the girls' bathroom, drop my books on the octagon tiles of the cold floor, frantically turn water on, slosh it crazily over my mouth, trying to wash away the tobacco taste, his saliva mingled with mine. I must never tell anyone, my parents must never know. They would think it was my fault, would not believe that a man who lives in our neighborhood and has been to our church would do such a thing. Somehow I brought this on myself. I must live with the secret, must hide it in my dresser drawer beneath my underwear with my little five-year diary, safe from everyone.

I go to Home Room. The girl is there selling defense stamps. More humiliation. I can't afford to buy even one. *But they only cost a dime!* she says perkily. She never gives up, tough and patriotic, smug in her saddle shoes and short plaid pleated skirt, the sleeves of her bulky sweater correctly pushed up to the elbows. She can't believe I won't show up one of these Fridays with a dime to help win the war. I am a great challenge to her, the only person in Home Room 305 who has never bought a defense stamp. At least she doesn't seem to guess that Mr. Dickson has kissed me.

First hour I can go to Latin, blessed class where I can lose myself in Mrs. Halvorsen's smile of approval when I read aloud. She calls on me and as soon as I stand up, my book in hand, I am back in the old Roman days, happy with Caesar, the folds of his toga soft and friendly as Jesus's robes in old Sunday School picture books. But when I swallow, before I go on to the next sentence, I get a sudden taste of tobacco, feel his saliva in my mouth. I have to stop reading, have to tell Mrs. Halvorsen I don't feel well. Have to sit down or leave the room. Inside my head a great roaring and I sense them all now as one and the same—Julius Caesar, Jesus, Mr. Dickson, and my father. Yes, even my father.

HARRIET

She winds her hair in perfect pin curls,
flattens them against her small head.
She bathes in lilac-scented bathwater,
talcums her breasts under the kimono
he brought home from Japan after his Navy years.

She waits now for him,
driving his truck across South Dakota.
Her meat loaf and baked potatoes
wait in the reliable Monarch oven;
her hands wait, leafing through magazines
rich with promises, and her hair waits
for the comb to caress it into deep waves
black against her face
soft and white with Coty's powder.

When the doorbell rings,
she is afraid to answer.
She wants no sound now except
his familiar, *Anybody home?*
She always laughs when he calls out.
Where would I ever be, honey,
but right here, waiting for you?

She goes to the door with reluctant steps
to find his best friend,
face red and splitting
like a late-garden radish,
smiling his body into their house.
I've come to keep you company, he says,
until he comes back.

Later she runs to our house next door,
hair falling from pin curls,
choking out words about a man
who has *done something bad to her.*
Her husband will never believe
she didn't want that red face buried
in her powdered breasts.

I promise to stay with her
until her husband returns, and
together we walk
across the crumbling fall garden,
together we go through the tiny house,
lock every door, latch every window,
as though we can lock out her fear,
or the suspicion now entering the husband
as he drives across the Dakota plains,
pressing his accelerator flat
to bring him swiftly home.

MOVIE STAR

On the radio we hear the news:
Jean Harlow is dead.
We sit in the darkened living room
of our neighbor's house,
the Olsons', their shades
pulled against heat and grief.

The Olson girls sit crying
on their davenport,
tears dropping
on their *Photoplays*.
They hold the key
to my life, their shades
always pulled,
their living room
like the womb
of the many movie houses
I yearn for
but am never allowed to enter.
And they wear lipstick,
forbidden scarlet cream,
as though they were movie stars.
I watch them stroke the tubes
of Tangee across their lips,
their mouths bleeding
into bloom in their mirrors.
I dream of movielands
blooming beyond the cornstalks
unfolding outside in the July heat.

Joy Olson stands beside me
in the fourth grade picture,
her hair blonde and frizzy as Harlow's,
her mouth ready for stardom,
while her heavy-lidded eyes
already seem to know
that the boy standing
in the row above her
will leave a baby in her
by the end of the movie.

RUMBLE SEAT

Yesterday in the antique store
I walked into a pale peach chiffon dress,
like the one Darlene Oakwig wore
for her confirmation in 1935,
an antique dress now, but brand new then
and store-bought with cape sleeves, bias cut,
draped softly over her white arms,
skirt with scalloped hem that dipped
and rose against her slender legs
in silk stockings for the first time.
She lives still in my father's attic
where the pictures from his confirmation classes
lie stacked next to his old theology books.
This morning she calls to me from behind
the wet stones of the old houses I pass
on my morning walk down Summit Avenue,
her hair in soft waves,
finger waves we called them,
formed by fingers dipped in thick clear lotion.
My girl friends and I yearned to know how
to do it, envied the older girls like Darlene
with curves of hair swooping down around
her bland impassive face in the confirmation picture,
her eyes movie-star languid, her mouth impatient.
I watched her from afar, a child mild and obedient,
and later I heard the grownups whisper how she
had grown wild, like the wildness of my own daughter at sixteen
going out with the twenty-seven-year-old punk rock singer.
Darlene Oakwig rode in rumble seats with boys
from Hector and Clarkfield, towns only a few miles
down the road from Sacred Heart, but foreign and strange
to us, dark with mystery and wickedness.
She rode away from her confirmation vows
to renounce the Devil and all his works and ways,
rode away to drink beer and laugh loudly with rough, older boys
in rumble seats, uncovered passenger seats that opened
out from the rear of their cars, not family cars
with safely-enclosed back seats, but wild roughneck cars,

open to the wind, gravel spitting into their laughing mouths.
Darlene Oakwig, killed in a car crash coming home
from a dance in Hector, her gravestone next to our family's
in the little cemetery on the outskirts of town,
Darlene Oakwig, far older than me, her eyes
in the confirmation picture already seeing
what I have not yet looked upon.

Alone in the house. She used to crave that solitary confinement, longed for the day when the kids would all be in school, her husband safely off to his job, and she would be alone in the house. At last she had achieved her desire. Desire. What meaning did that word have any more? Desirelessness was the goal of Zen Buddhists, her friend who sat at the Zen Center had told her. Her hand itched. She paused to scratch it slowly, languorously, meditatively. Red welts appeared. *Welts?* What exactly were welts anyway? She pulled down her trusty *American Heritage Dictionary*. Booker T. Washington. There he was right above George. Taliaferro was his middle name. Where did his mother ever get that? Born in 1856 and died in 1915. She wanted to know more about him. Peanuts, something about peanuts, right? No, that was George Washington Carver. 1864? to 1943, American agricultural chemist and educator. Not to know the exact date of your birth! They'd told her to eat peanuts during the time she'd had those tests. Every day for three days she'd had to bring in stool samples and hand them over to the brisk and totally-well nurse behind the desk. But of course she wasn't really a nurse. Just a lackey. Wonder what a *lackey* really is. Back to the ls. She'd no idea that *lampreys* were so snakelike. There was a picture of one and the description was utterly repellent: *primitive elongated fishes, having a jawless sucking mouth with rasping tongue*. There was a closeup detail of the mouth. It looked like a vagina. Back a few years when *Our Bodies, Ourselves* had first come out, she'd followed the suggestion to take a tiny mirror and examine her vagina. She was sorry she'd done it. Not a pretty sight, a vagina, no matter what Judy Chicago said. Flower-like indeed. Why pretend? What fun must it be for gynecologists? Certainly it must deaden their desires. That word again. The fleshy part of her hand itched now. Right under her thumb. She scratched it vigorously. More welts. She'd never gotten to them. Back to *American Heritage*, faithful red friend. Bunch of Commies was what she and her friends had been called that Saturday before Easter years ago, way back in 1958 it must've been, because her son was only two and still in a stroller. *Go back to where you came from*, someone standing outside of Daytons had actually said, and spat upon her. Who'd think it? In front of Daytons at that. Welts, welts. Use the guide words. *Weeping willow*. Her father said he'd planted that for her. *A tree for each of you children, and for you, I'll plant a weeping willow because you cry so much*. She hadn't thought it was fair, didn't think she hardly ever cried, especially then, before her mother died. Except that time when she was three and the darling only child, before her brother was born, and they'd driven her over to Ringsven Studio in Granite Falls to have her picture taken in the strange room with one whole wall painted to look like the forest Hansel and Gretel had gotten lost in – she'd recognized it at once. She'd been afraid the person under the black cloth was really the oven-witch in disguise, and cried and cried and refused to sit as she was asked to do with one leg tucked under her buttock. Her father had taken her out back of the studio, where the Minnesota River ran sluggish and brown below, and spanked her again and again, giving her, as he'd said, something to really cry about. She'd stared at the picture many times since then and could find no trace of tears on that angelic child face, the soft blonde hair curled with the hot iron, the elaborately-ruffled dress and bonnet. The welts. They were rising again. She was scratching without realizing it, the soft inside of her left arm, scratching aimlessly, but relentlessly, digging deeper and deeper. Here it was at last: *welt, a ridge or bump raised on the skin by a lash or blow or sometimes by an allergic disorder.* He'd hit her many times, over and over again, about the shoulders, kicked her on her legs, punched her in the breasts, always careful not to strike her anywhere that would show the next day. Because she had to go to work. He didn't want her to lose her job. They needed the money. He had expensive tastes. Before they'd flown to San Juan for their winter vacation, he'd gone out and bought sets of matched luggage, real leather. He'd hidden the American Express bill, but she'd found it, months later, still unpaid, stuck behind a cup of pencils on his desk, the antique roll top for which he'd paid over a thousand dollars. A real buy, he'd told her. A steal. He used to talk like that, like a hustler, a travelling salesman. Except he never travelled without her. Mostly he stayed home. He wanted to keep track of her. When he came down to breakfast in the morning, he never remembered what he'd done. *What are those things on your legs?* he'd ask, angry again. He wanted her to be perfect. *Welts,* she'd say. *Welts.*

CHEVVY

So when I started going out with John,
he couldn't believe I didn't know how to drive.
We rode around in an old Chevvy with no heater;
John was a Stoic, graduate student in philosophy
who didn't believe in romantic love, in flattering
women with compliments or flowers or opening car doors,
believed way back in 1953 women should be independent,
so he insisted I learn to drive.
We spent endless hours tooling around Lake Nokomis,
safe on its low-speed-limit parkways,
and I was getting the hang of it,
getting even to enjoy it,
until that day he decided it was time for me
to pull out into real traffic.
When I stopped at the Cedar Avenue stop sign,
I waited, waited some more, kept waiting, began to ease out,
pulled back, terrified, until finally I broke down
in tears, got out of the driver's seat,
walked around to his side, beseeched him
to take the wheel.
He refused at first, disgusted by my tears,
but finally drove us home.

I never got into the driver's seat again
until twenty years later, after all three of our kids
were born and I went back to teaching,
got a charge account,
hired a man young enough to be my son,
who called me by first name,
cajoled me into going out on the freeway,
got me ready to pass the test.
Of course you can do it, Phebe,
he kept telling me,
and I've been driving ever since.

POLICEMAN

To go off alone, to shuck it all, to hit the road, to leave the dailies behind where poems disappear, die in labor, deaf to the pen's mouth-to-mouth resuscitation. The hero hits the road, doesn't wave goodbye, leaves no notes of instruction to the children, admonitions to be good, pleas for understanding, never feels guilt, acts without regret. But I cannot leave, for even were I to go to the ends of the earth, or were I to descend to the bottom of the ocean and be swallowed by the whale, he would follow me, he would be there, the father, the pointing finger, the sudden siren, the policeman calling me to the curb at two a.m: *Ma'am, have you any idea why we have stopped you? Do you realize what you have done? Do you understand?* The unpaid phone bill for too many calls in the middle of the night? The letter never written to my aunt before she died of a heart attack in a little rooming house in Norway? The papers of students lying unread in the dark of my briefcase? My back turned to him in bed, dreaming of a radio pushed into his bath water? I look up, feigning innocence. *No, I do not, sir.* He is not going to get me. I will not give in. I will lie and lie before I give in, before I cry out again as I did that night at Bible Camp kneeling at the pew with all the other high school girls, the evangelist's hand moving across our hair, the evangelist dropping the Holy Spirit on the soft hair of all those kneeling, ecstatic girls, reaching over in the rowboat to hand me a water lily, kissing me full on my earthly lips, the horror and joy of fleshly desire, the ecstatic moment in the dour religion of Jesus. Yes, I am guilty, I have sinned, o father forgive me, here is my body, given for you. I have written checks with insufficient funds, have sat alone in rooms writing when I should have offered myself to him. Instead of sinking my hands deep into garden dirt or bread dough, I have moved them across the pages of blank books, the little teeth of my fountain pen casting hard shadows across the white flesh of the page. *You have a perfect driving record. It would be a shame to spoil that. We'll let you go. This time.*

JEALOUSY

She writes my husband notes,
signs them 48-24-36;
her black hair licks his ears
as they kiss by my sink.
Before supper she bakes bread
with sunflower seeds and nuts.
Ten loaves warm on the counter.
She irons shirts and even sheets,
smooth and white as her thighs.
She reads *Remembrance of Things Past*,
their heads bent over the same copy.
She learns to play chess
without being coaxed; he teaches
her all the moves in one hour.
Every morning she runs around
the lake with him, climbs into
his tub when they return.
Now she is in bed between us;
her breasts take up all the room.

divorce ?

DRIVE-IN

After the poetry reading in Faribault,
I drive home on the straight freeway,
fields of snow on either side and signs
which proclaim: NO DRIVING ON SHOULDERS,
and I remember your body,
asleep alone now in our old bed,
how I used to lean on your shoulder
as we drove home from drive-in movies,
our children asleep in the back seat,
hard wheels spinning, whirling into gravel,
as we slipped off the freeway
onto the soft shoulder,
where we sat together in the hazy light,
looked out into the dark soil
of spring-plowed fields
waiting for the first frail shoots of corn.

WHY I HAVE SIMPLIFIED MY LIFE

Due to improper handling,
that's what Terry,
my personal banker,
said when she wrote to tell me
she was closing down
my checking account,
but it's all right, Terry,
I've learned to work with cash,
come to prefer it actually,
those one hundred dollar bills
I always ask for
when I cash my pay check.
No one can ever change them,
and they simplify things
when one of the kids
asks for a couple of dollars.
I've given up my car, too,
or rather it's given up me,
and I always take the bus
or walk or drive my new
unfashionable three-speed bike.
My daughter doesn't want to be seen
with me, says I ride too low in the seat,
look like I'm on
one of those adult tricycles.
I've given up cigarettes, too,
way back on September 4, 1979,
at 11 a.m. I decided never to smoke again,
because I heard that my doctor,
my age and fat and healthy like me,
even though a terrific smoker,
had dropped dead of a stroke
while making her hospital rounds.
The things I've given up to simplify my life:
plans to read all the novels of Henry James,
to finish *Moby Dick* and *Middlemarch*;
I've given up ironing, meal preparation,
and most housework;

I've allowed my subscription to the *Village Voice*
and *The New Yorker* to expire,
along with the satisfaction
of having my finger on the pulse
of the New York art and literary scene.
I've had to give up my father,
who went to join my mother, sister, and brother
in that cemetery outside Sacred Heart, Minnesota,
one snowy November day.
Now that I've lost my last buffer against death,
there probably isn't anything
I can't learn to get along without.

KING TUT

At the slide lecture in the Field Museum
we listen to the earnest Art History grad student
prepare us for the King Tut exhibit:
When they lifted the gold mask
from Tutankhaman's face,
the skin, penetrated by an overzealous
application of precious ointments and unguents,
fell away from his bones.

After the lecture,
after examining the fifty-five objects
placed in the king's tomb
to accompany him on his journey
to the afterlife,
I go to my hotel to bathe.
I have appalled the docent
from the Minneapolis Institute of Arts
by telling her I've come on this tour
mainly because we are staying
at the Palmer House,
only hotel I've ever found
whose bathtubs are deep enough
to satisfy my longing
to be totally immersed
in steaming water until my skin
reddens with bliss.

Lying in the tub,
I remember the slide showing the sarcophagus
from which they lifted King Tut's mummy
which had lain undisturbed for over three thousand years.
The thirsting of the flesh to live forever,
to keep the husks of skin covering the bones.
I remember my minister father
standing in his pulpit as he preached
the sermon at the funeral
of a young mother whose heart hadn't lasted
through the surgery to repair it:

This body is only a shell. The real person
has flown home to be with God.
Her baby whimpered in the father's arms,
hungry for milk from the body whose profile
was faintly visible above the rim of the casket.

I run my soapy hands up and down
the familiar mounds of my body,
inspecting them for signs of decay,
and remember how as a child I used to
bend over my knees
to examine the shiny pink skin
revealed under the rough scabs
from roller skating falls,
how I used to wonder at the body's
endless recreation of new skin.

Soon I swathe myself in the hotel's huge white towels,
lie down on the firm mattress until I am dry,
then unwind myself from the towels as I rise,
as I used to imagine the dead would come forth
from their graves on Resurrection Day,
trailing their tattered coffin garments behind them
as they flew upward into the clouds
to meet Jesus.

I rub Johnson's baby oil
into my knees and elbows, obeying
TV commercial instructions to keep my skin smooth,
using precious ointments and sweet-smelling unguents,
preparing myself for another miraculous appearance
on Wabash Avenue,
faithful knees still bending and unbending,
to keep it alive,
my body, my life's work.

Phebe Hanson spent her childhood in the little farming community of Sacred Heart, Minnesota, during the great depression of the thirties. She attended Augsburg College, taught high school English for several years in small towns in western Minnesota, married and settled down in Minneapolis to raise three children. In the late sixties she began teaching again and discovered Women Poets of the Twin Cities, a group of women who encouraged her to write poetry. She currently teaches at the Minneapolis College of Art and Design. She is a 1985 Bush Fellow.

13
- 11
- 17
- 27
41